MOTHER
AFRICA

My mother takes very good care of me.

She feeds me when I am hungry.

She gives me water to drink.

She gives me clothes to wear.

She gives me shelter to protect me.

She loves me, and I love her.

There is no love like my mother's love.

My mother talks to me daily.

I hear her voice when
I just need my mother.

My mother is strong!

Especially when she needs to be strong.

My mother cares for me and shows it in so many ways.

Africa is my mother.

I love her, and she LOVES me!

Who do you love?

Who loves you?